# VIZ MANGA SAMPLER
## 2019

# Introduction

VIZ Media has an excellent lineup of manga series for 2019. This year our offerings include a *My Hero Academia* parody, the long-awaited continuation of *JoJo's Bizarre Adventure*, highly anticipated Shojo Beat romances, a critically acclaimed anthropomorphic high school tale, Rumiko Takahashi's iconic rom-com *Urusei Yatsura* and more. We hope you enjoy this sampler of some of our favorite new series.

# TABLE OF CONTENTS

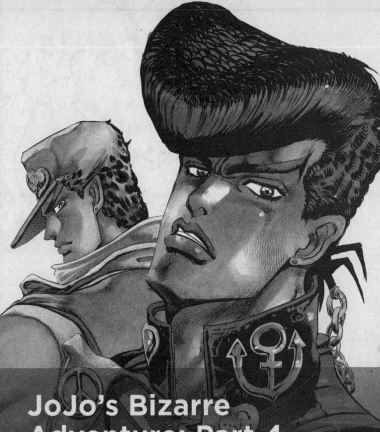

# JoJo's Bizarre Adventure: Part 4—Diamond Is Unbreakable

Story and Art by Hirohiko Araki

The multigenerational tale of the heroic Joestar family and their never-ending battle against evil continues!

In April 1999, Jotaro Kujo travels to a town in Japan called Morioh to find a young man named Josuke Higashikata, the secret love child of his grandfather, Joseph Joestar. Upon finding him, Jotaro is surprised to learn that Josuke also possesses a Stand. After their strange meeting, the pair team up to investigate the town's proliferation of unusual Stands!

ニヤリ
GRIN

LISTEN UP, OKUYASU...

...

UR...
K...

... 

IT DOESN'T MATTER HOW FAST THE MACHINE CAN GO IF A *CLUMSY, GUTLESS DIMWIT* IS COWERING BEHIND THE WHEEL WITH HIS FOOT OFF THE GAS.

USING A STAND IS LIKE DRIVING A CAR OR A MOTORCYCLE—

JOSUKE HIGASHIKATA BESTED ANGELO. YOU *WILL* KILL HIM! NO MORE EXCUSES!

JUST THINKING OF THE *TERRIFIC POWER* OF YOUR STAND— *THE HAND*—IS ENOUGH TO MAKE EVEN ME QUAKE... SO USE IT *PROPERLY!*

THIS ISN'T A GAME, *OKUYASU!*

YOU DON'T NEED TO COME DOWN SO HARD ON ME, BRO.

THIS PUNK JUST MOVES FASTER THAN I EXPECTED, THAT'S ALL.

YES, I—

KOICHI!

I TOLD YOU TO GET OUT OF MY WAY.

THANK GOODNESS, YOU'RE STILL ALIVE.

I CAN STILL SAVE YOU—

FWUMP

DOOOOOM

BILLION

IT'S ONLY A HUNCH, BUT I THINK I'D BETTER WATCH OUT FOR THAT HAND.

THIS GUY... HE KEEPS SWINGING WITH THE SAME ARM—LIKE HE THINKS ALL HE HAS TO DO IS LAY HIS RIGHT HAND ON ME.

?!

SO. THERE IS SOMETHING ABOUT THAT HAND!

LET GO OF MY RIGHT HAND, ASSHOLE!

OOF!

URK!

WHAT HAPPENED TO YOU MANGLING MY ARM? OR WAS THAT ALL JUST TALK?

OR ARE YOU GOING TO LEAVE YOUR FRIEND TO DIE?

DON'T YOU TRY TO RUN, JOSUKE!

KOICHI... I NEED YOU TO HANG ON A LITTLE LONGER.

...

YOU CAN FIGURE IT OUT AFTER YOU'RE DEAD! NOW LET'S DO THIS, YOU SON OF A BITCH.

BUT SOMETHING TELLS ME IT'S SERIOUSLY DANGEROUS.

I DON'T KNOW WHAT'S SO SPECIAL ABOUT YOUR RIGHT HAND...

SIGN ON GATE: NO PASSING

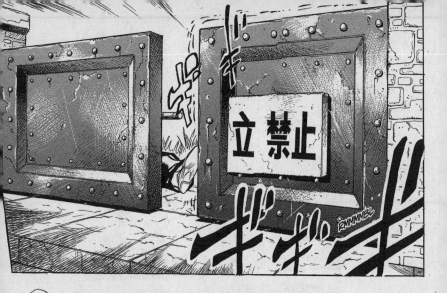

NO... PASSING?

WHAT THE HELL?

SOME- THING'S OFF... DIFFERENT THAN BEFORE.

THAT GATE...

YOU'RE GETTING FARTHER AWAY FROM YOUR PRECIOUS FRIEND, YOU KNOW.

KEEPING YOUR DISTANCE, SMART GUY?

WHY DON'T YOU COME A LITTLE CLOSER INSTEAD?

YOUR STAND'S RIGHT HAND DID THAT.

WHERE'D THE OTHER LETTERS GO?

立禁止

YOUR STAND CAN CARVE AWAY PHYSICAL SPACE!

IT CUT OUT PART OF THE GATE.

IF YOU'RE WONDERING WHERE THE ERASED PARTS GO...

ANYTHING MY STAND'S RIGHT HAND GRASPS WILL BE *CARVED AWAY.*

THE PARTS LEFT BEHIND CLOSE TOGETHER *JUST AS THEY WERE BEFORE.* BUT!

THAT'S RIGHT, JOSUKE!

EVEN I DON'T KNOW WHERE THEY END UP.

AND I CAN DO *THIS* TO BASTARDS WHO THINK THEY CAN ESCAPE ME!

NOW YOU DIE!

DOOM

WOULD YOU LOOK AT THAT! YOU CAME RIGHT TO ME... JUST LIKE *TELEPORTING!*

UZZZSHT

HUH?!

YOU'RE NOT TOO BRIGHT, ARE YOU?

JUST AS I THOUGHT...

More in **JoJo'**s ... **art 4—** ...nd Is Unbrea...

# Kakuriyo: Bed & Breakfast for Spirits

Art by Waco Ioka
Original Story by Midori Yuma
Character Design by Laruha

Aoi Tsubaki inherited her grandfather's ability to see spirits—
and his massive debt to them! Now she's been kidnapped and
taken to Kakuriyo, the spirit world, to make good on his bill. Her
options: marry the head of the inn her grandfather trashed, or
get eaten by demons. But Aoi isn't the type to let spirits push her
around, and she's determined to redeem her grandfather's IOU
on her own terms!

GRANDPA PASSED AWAY...

...ABOUT A MONTH AGO.

WOMEN USED TO THROW THEM-SELVES AT HIM.

MOVIE TICKET STUBS.

PAPER-BACKS WITH SUN-DAMAGED COVERS.

I have no idea...

IS THIS AN OFUDA?

HE WAS WHAT MOST PEOPLE WOULD CALL A WASTE OF SPACE.

HE HAD LOVERS EVERYWHERE, AND FATHERED AN UNBELIEVABLE NUMBER OF CHILDREN.

GRANDPA DIDN'T HAVE A STEADY JOB. HE WANDERED ALL OVER JAPAN.

I STILL THINK HE WAS A GREAT MAN.

THERE WAS SUCH A LONG, LONG LINE OF PEOPLE...

...WHO'D COME TO MOURN HIM.

BLACK AND WHITE PHOTOS...

IT WAS LIKE...

...A YOKAI PARADE FROM A PICTURE SCROLL.

...ayed at an inn in ...ryo and made a very ...ortant promise. ...t forget, since it

TENJIN-YA?

HE WAS REALLY HANDSOME.

There's this aura around him.

IT LOOKS LIKE THIS PHOTO WAS TAKEN IN FRONT OF A JAPANESE INN.

A REALLY OLD ONE.

tenjin-ya

OH!

GRANDPA!

HE'S SO YOUNG HERE, MAYBE ABOUT MY AGE?

Wow!

WAIT A SEC.

FINE.

GNH...

SNAP

!!

**Brown Rice Balls**
*Stuffed with chopped cucumber and miso chicken*

THEY'RE CUTE, BUT SOMETIMES THEY'RE SO PUSHY THEY PISS ME OFF.

THIS BIG ONE'S MINE.

THERE'S CUCUMBER IN THEM!

YAAAAY!!

RICE BALLS.

HMM? OH?

WHAT'S WRONG WITH YOU?

ONLY THE STRONGEST SURVIVE IN THIS WORLD.

GLOOM

SHP

I WISH THERE WAS A SIGN...

...SAYING "DON'T FEED THE KAPPA"...

SIGH

HE COULDN'T GRAB ANYTHING TO EAT.

THANK YOU SO MUCH!

HERE.

YOU CAN HAVE MY RICE BALL.

RUMMAGE

LITTLE LIAR...

SHE MUST BE CRAZY.

THERE'S NO ONE THERE.

I WAS ALWAYS ALONE.

THIS IS DELICIOUS.

HE COULD SEE AYAKASHI TOO, BUT HE DIDN'T CARE WHAT PEOPLE THOUGHT OF HIM.

MY GRAND-FATHER RESCUED ME FROM THAT LONELINESS.

I DEAL WITH AYAKASHI BY FEEDING THEM.

GRANDPA WAS NOTORIOUS AMONG THE AYAKASHI...

HUNGRY AYAKASHI TRY TO DEVOUR THE HUMANS WHO CAN SEE THEM.

AND I'M A FREQUENT TARGET.

...AND I WAS DRAGGED INTO ALL KINDS OF TROUBLE BECAUSE OF HIM.

THAT'S WHY I GIVE THEM HOME-COOKED MEALS.

MUNCH

MUNCH

YOU ARE A STRANGE HUMAN, AOI.

IT HELPS ME AVOID GETTING ATTACKED...

YOU ARE THE ONLY HUMAN WHO FEEDS AYAKASHI.

THERE AREN'T MANY HUMANS WHO CAN SEE AYAKASHI IN THE FIRST PLACE.

THOSE WHO CAN USUALLY TRY TO EXORCISE US.

I'D DO THAT TOO...

SIGH...

...IF I HAD THE POWER.

YOU WOULD NEVER DO THAT, AOI.

I KNOW YOU WOULDN'T.

HUNGER IS A MISERABLE THING.

I CAN'T STAND TO SEE ANYONE, HUMAN OR AYAKASHI, GO HUNGRY.

HEY.

YOU'RE HUNGRY, RIGHT?

I DON'T WANT TO LISTEN TO YOU WHINING ABOUT IT.

DO YOU WANT THIS? IT'S MY LUNCH.

AND I DON'T WANT YOU ATTACKING HUMANS BECAUSE YOU NEED TO EAT.

SHUU

SHA

SLSSH

## ~ Menu ~

- Ginger-fried pork with pickled plums
- Soy braised lotus root
- Mustard greens with bonito soy sauce
- Mushroom stir fry
- Savory omelet roll with green onions
- White rice with pickled daikon

CLIK

IS THIS A YOUNG MALE AYAKASHI?

THANK YOU.

...

BING BONG

HMM, WHERE'S MY LUNCH BOX...?

AH, FOUND IT.

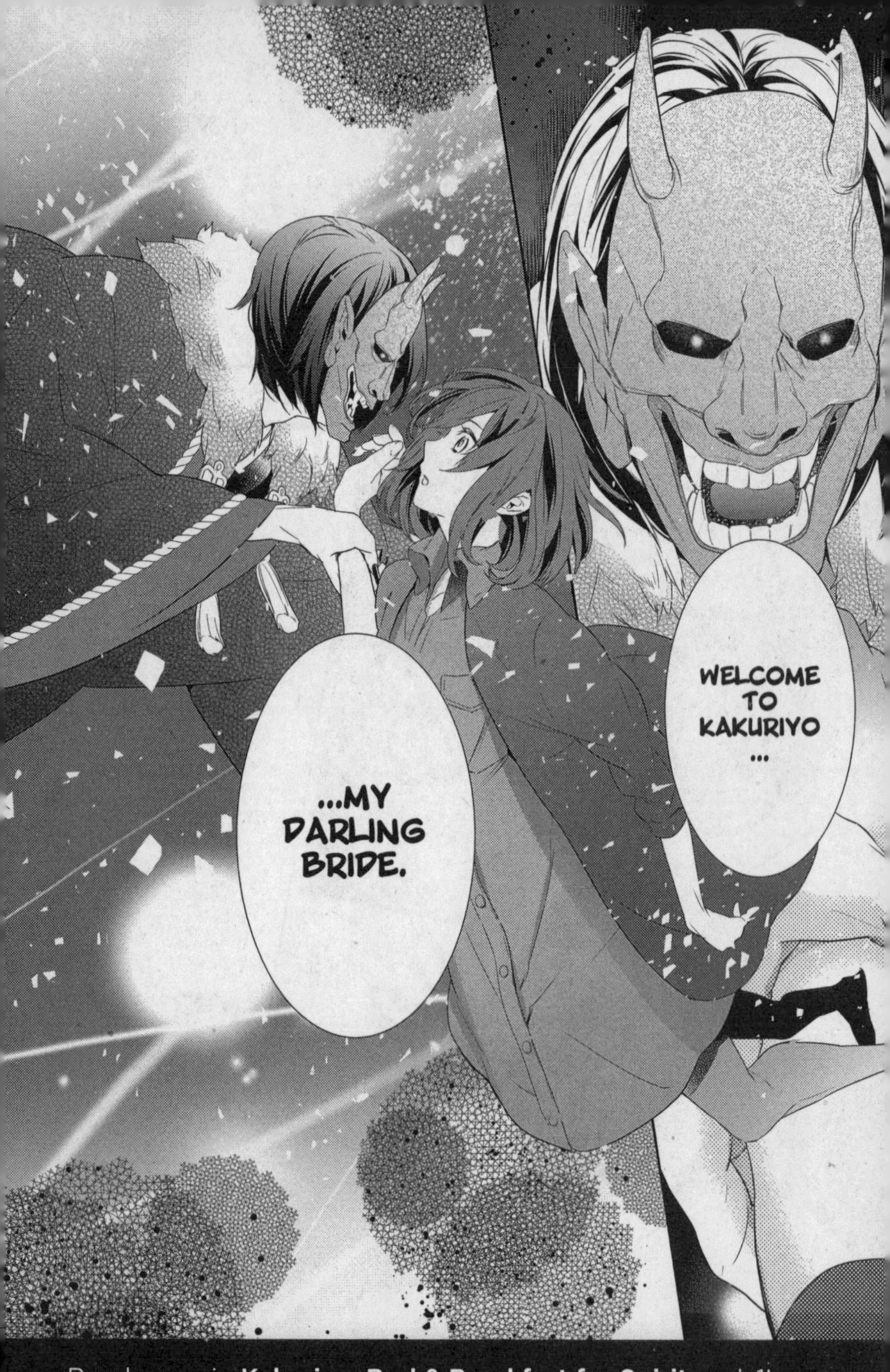
WELCOME TO KAKURIYO ...
...MY DARLING BRIDE.

# Komi Can't Communicate

Story and Art by Tomohito Oda

Socially anxious high school student Shoko Komi's greatest dream is to make some friends, but everyone at school mistakes her crippling social anxiety for cool reserve! With the whole student body keeping their distance and Komi unable to utter a single word, friendship might be forever beyond her reach.

TODAY, I STARTED HIGH SCHOOL.

Next, assemble in the gym!

Bow!

On your feet!

MY NAME IS HITOHITO TADANO.

...IS TO NOT MAKE WAVES.

KOMIIIII

MY GOAL AS A HIGH SCHOOL STUDENT...

THOK

?!

I'M NORMAL IN EVERY WAY, SO IT'S THE PERFECT OBJECTIVE FOR—

...that was his plan.

I love you!

Are you on LINE?

Komi!!

Where do you live?

At least...

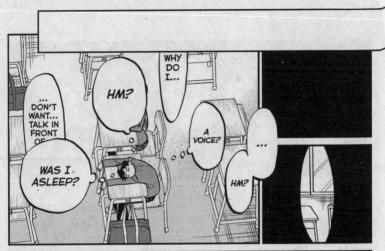

ARE YOU...

...NOT VERY GOOD AT TALKING TO PEOPLE?

WHAT AM I SAYING?!

SHTMP

Communication 4 — The End

How did you know that I'm bad at talking to people?

No.

HUH? WELL...

...I JUST SENSED IT.

HASN'T ANYONE ELSE EVER NOTICED?

...REALLY?

...UM...

OH...

...RUN OUT OF STUFF TO TALK ABOUT!

WE'VE ALREADY...

I CAN'T STAND THIS!

!

Tadano took flight.

SO I BETTER GET GOING!

AGH!

W-WE'RE SUP- POSED TO BE IN THE GYM!

Wait.

UH...

But he couldn't get away!!

W-w- w-w-w- w-w-w- w-w-w- w-w-w- w-w-w- w-w-w- w-w-w- w-w-w- w-w-w- w-w-w- w-w-w- w-w-w- w-w-w- w-w-w- w-w-w- w...

SHAKE SHAKE SHAKE SHAKE SHAKE SHAKE SHAKE SHAKE

W-w- w-w-w- w-w-w- w-w-w- w-w-w- w-w-w- w-w-w- w-w-w- w-w-w- w-w-w- w-w-w- w-w-w- w-w-w- w-w...

DOES SHE WANT TO TALK ABOUT SOMETHING?

SKIRK SKIRK

I couldn't finish my lunch.

i couldn't finish my lunch.

...?! ...?

SO... YOU'RE HUNGRY?

Actually, I want to talk.

?  ?

OH...

But actually I want to talk.

I get nervous in front of people. My face freezes up and I get scared.

Or they kneel and bow.

Or they run away or pass out.

People get uneasy around me.

GLOOM

SHE'S GOT IT SO WRONG...

I know that.

I think they hate me.

I'm certain they do. Because I'm so difficult to talk to.

TRMBL

I had a hard time eating
by myself at lunch.

And watching everyone
chat as they ate.

It hurt.

Every day for
three years I tried
to join.

In
junior
high

But
I couldn't
speak.      No matter
how hard
I tried.

I just
couldn't
speak.

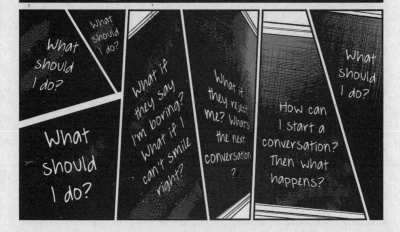

What should I do?

What
should
I do?

What
should
I do?

What if
they say
I'm boring?
What if I
can't smile
right?

What if
they reject
me? What's
the next
conversation
?

How can
I start a
conversation?
Then what
happens?

What
should
I do?

Communication 5 — The End

Komi Can't

Communicate

Sorry.

Your hiccups ...

DID THEY STOP?

I can't talk about it

What's fun & what makes me happy & my failures & schoolwork & what was on TV last night & the weather...

Other people can do it, but I can't.

I can't even say hello.

↓ Sorta happy

SH-SHE...

...SAID MY NAME!

How can I make it up to you?

I'm bothering you, Tadano.

I'm sorry.

HUH?

I'm sorry.

THOK

DID YOU DO SOMETHING TO APOLOGIZE FOR?

I don't remember.

SHE BLEW OFF MY QUESTION!

Anyway

Sorry for talking too much.

I'm sorry.

Anyway, I wanted to apologize.

Just forget about all of this.

Sorry for talking too much.

Goodbye.

SKRIK

SKRIK

Isn't the weather nice today?

The cherry blossoms were beautiful.

Let's try some more...

Heart-beat

To make 100 friends.

What's your dream, Komi?

Please don't laugh.

Then I'll be your first friend and help you make 99 more.

HUFFF

SKRIK

SKRIK

? TENSE

SKRIK

SWIF SWUF

S-S-SORRY!! PRETTY OBNOXIOUS, RIGHT?! ME?! YOUR FIRST FRIEND?! SORRY! I JUST GOT CARRIED AWAY!!

Then, I'll be your first friend and help you make 99 more.

Then, I'll be your first friend and help you make 99 more.

BLUSH

# Sounds good.

HUH?

THUS, THE CURTAIN ROSE ON MY UNORDINARY HIGH SCHOOL LIFE.

Communication 6 — The End

Which means you need *personality!*

Itan Private High School is an elite prep school, but the entrance exam is *an interview!* (Paper tests are just conducted for appearance's sake.)

Tadano hasn't realized!!

...has a very high concentration of quirky individuals!!

ECCENTRICS!

OUTSIDERS!

WEIRDOS!

FREAKS!

So this school...

...KOMI!

OH... ...GOOD MORNING...

And Tadano hasn't realized...

...how difficult it will be for Komi to make friends here.

...

... mff.

TREMMMMM

Goo... Goo... Googoo googoo good momo momo morrr...

MMMMMB LE

# Komi Can't

# Communicate

**Communication 7: One More Time**

K-KOMI!

SHIINE

BASICALLY, SHE GLOWS.

HOW- EVER...

"LET'S BE FRIENDS."

TRY SAYING...

F-FIRST, LET'S PRACTICE SPEAKING!

IF YOU CAN SAY THAT, THEN YOU'LL MAKE 100 FRIENDS IN NO TIME!

P'WIK

!

Communication 7 — The End

Tadano decided that his goal in high school is to help Komi make a hundred friends.

The story thus far...

EVERYONE ADMIRES HER, SO THIS SHOULD BE EASY.

NOW WHO DO I TALK TO?

I'VE VISUALIZED MY SUCCESS!

...AND THEY'LL ALL JUMP AT THE CHANCE!

KOMI WANTS TO HAVE FRIENDS!

I'LL TELL OUR CLASS-MATES...

Yay! We're gonna be friends!!

AH HA HA

GLANCE

GLANCE

!

AHHHH

...scumbag scumbag scumbag scumbag scumbag scumbag scumbag scumbag scumbag scumbag scumbag scumbag scumbag scumbag scumbag scumbag scumbag scumbag scumbag scumbag scumbag scumbag scumbag scumbag scumbag scumbag scumbag scumbag scumbag scumbag scumbag scumbag scumbag scumbag scumbag scumbag scumbag scumbag scumbag scumbag scumbag scumbag scumbag scumbag scumbag.

GRRRIP

Hunh?! What's your problem?! How dare you speak such a hallowed name?! Refer to her as "Her Highness," loser! Don't get presumptuous just because you sit next to her, scumbag! I saw you talking to her before class, but do you know what a miracle that is?! You're less than horse poop, so be thankful you breathe the same air as her, you arrogant scumbag

So, what do you need?

PERK

Tadano realized he was in a tough position.

Then stop talking to me.

Oh. really?

FOR-GET I EVER—

UH, NOTH-ING.

## Communication 8 — The End

Read more in **Komi**

# My Hero Academia: Smash!!

**Story and Art by Hirofumi Neda**
**Original Concept by Kohei Horikoshi**

The superpowered society of *My Hero Academia* takes a hilarious turn in this reimagining of the best-selling series! Join Midoriya, All Might and all the aspiring heroes of U.A. High, plus memorable villains, in an irreverent take on the main events of the series, complete with funny gags, ridiculous jokes and superpowered humor!

## WITH GREAT POWER COMES A GREAT DISCLAIMER

MY QUIRK IS THE ABILITY TO **TRANSFER** POWER.

THE FIRST CULTIVATES THE POWER, THEN PASSES IT TO ANOTHER...AND THOSE WITH BRAVE AND TRUE HEARTS LINK TO FORM A CRYSTALLINE NETWORK OF POWER!!

ONE FOR ALL

I BELIEVE THAT YOU...

...ARE A WORTHY SUCCESSOR!!

?!

DO I HAVE A REASON **NOT** TO ACCEPT? NO...

I HAVE NO REASON TO REFUSE!

YES... I ACCEPT.

INCIDENTALLY, IF YOUR LIMP-NOODLE BODY ISN'T READY FOR THE POWER, YOUR LIMBS WILL POP RIGHT OFF.

SO, COULD YOU JUST SIGN THIS WAVER?

TH-THAT'S SOME SERIOUS FINE PRINT!

CONTRACT

HIS EXISTENCE ALONE IS A DETERRENT TO VILLAINY...

HE'S A MAN WHO LIVES UP TO HIS NAME AS A "SYMBOL OF PEACE." AND THAT MAN SAID...

NO. 2!!

"YOU CAN BE A HERO."

BULGE

...

HOPING TO LIVE UP TO HIS MENTOR'S FAITH IN HIM, THE BOY SUMMONED THE COURAGE TO FACE BRUTAL TRAINING.

*HOW SHE IMAGINED IT.

## MACHIAVELLIAN

MY TRAINING STARTS WITH CLEANING UP?!

ALL THIS?!

HMM. THERE'S PLENTY HERE THAT JUST NEEDS A LITTLE SPIT-SHINE TO GET WORKING AGAIN.

OR, I COULD BREAK IT ALL DOWN INTO SALVAGEABLE MATERIALS...

I HEARD!! SOME OF IT'S HEAVY, BUT TOTALLY WORTH IT.

HIS STUFF IS STUPID CHEAP! YOU JUST HAVE TO HAUL IT HOME YOURSELF!

BEACH BAZAAR IZUKU

HRM... TALK ABOUT MISSING THE POINT.

I DID IT, ALL MIGHT.

A FEW DAYS LATER

SALE!!

## MANIFEST DESTINY

MY SELF-DESIGNED "PASS THE TEST, AMERICAN DREAM" PLAN!!

THAT'S WHAT THIS IS FOR!!

WITH BLISTERING RED EARTH AS FAR AS THE EYE COULD SEE, I FACED THE HELLISH HEAT AND PACKS OF COYOTES, ALL IN PURSUIT OF FREEDOM AND "GLORY"...

"HEAD WEST, YOUNG MAN," IT SAID, SO I DID.

A YET-UNDISCOVERED GIFT FROM THE GODS, GUSHING UP FROM THE GROUND...

THEN, ONE FATEFUL DAY, I FOUND IT.

FEELS LIKE I'M FORGETTING SOMETHING IMPORTANT...

...

FIFTY YEARS HAVE PASSED. NOWADAYS, I GAZE DOWN UPON THIS COUNTRY OF OURS FROM THE EXECUTIVE SUITE OF AN 80-STORY BUILDING.

American Dream Fulfilled!!

IZUKUOIL

MY HERO ACADEMIA - END.

## TWILIGHT ALL MIGHT!

PICK UP THE PACE, KID!! I'M GETTING OLD OVER HERE!

IN THE FLESH

HA HA HA

IT REALLY IS! NEVER SEEN HIM IN THE FLESH BEFORE!!

HEY, ISN'T THAT ALL MIGHT?!

HEY, WANNA COME PARTY WITH US?

WHOA THERE, LADIES. PLENTY OF ME TO GO AROUND.

ME TOO!

SQUEAL! ♥ CAN I HAVE YOUR AUTOGRAPH?

CAN I GET A SELFIE WITH YOU?

"MIDORIYA, KID, I'VE GOT SOME BUSINESS TO ATTEND TO. YOU CAN HANDLE THE REST OF THIS SERIES BY YOURSELF, RIGHT?"

SPLASH

ALL MIGHT

## PERTINENT POINT FOR PROS

THE YOUNG HEROES TODAY ONLY WANT FAME AND GLORY.

CRUNCH CRUNCH

NO MATTER HOW UNGLAM-OROUS! NEVER FORGET THAT.

BA M

BUT BEING A HERO IS ALL ABOUT VOLUNTEER WORK!

...ON YOUR PATH TO BECOMING A HERO!!

THIS IS THE FIRST STEP...

HE CRUSHED ALL MY THOUGHTS OF WRETCHED VAINGLORY ALONG WITH THAT FRIDGE.

TRMBL

I JUST HAPPENED TO BE PASSING BY, BUT HE REMINDED ME OF WHAT REALLY MATTERS.

ACK?!

3.5 MILLION YEN

*ABOUT $35,000

OH?

CAN YOU HELP ME OUT?

MOM, I NEED TO HAVE SPECIAL MEALS FOR TRAINING.

MEAL PLAN

YOWCH!

380 MILLION YEN

*ABOUT $3.8 MILLION

HE'S DILIGENT ENOUGH THAT THIS COULD REALLY WORK.

SO ELABORATE... I COULD AFFORD TO GO ON A DIET, SO MAYBE I'LL JOIN HIM?

900 MILLION YEN

UGH. THIS BIG CITY LIFE JUST ISN'T WORKING OUT!!

*ABOUT $9 MILLION

GREAT... MANAGED NOT TO PUKE MY GUTS OUT TODAY.

A FEW DAYS LATER

WELCOME HOME, KID.

PHEW

MAKE SURE OUR BABY GROWS UP BIG AND STRONG. ALSO, SEE THAT LIFE INSURANCE APPLICATION ON THE NIGHTSTAND...?

HI, I JUST WANTED TO HEAR YOUR VOICE...

H-HANG ON! YOU'VE GOT PLENTY TO LIVE FOR!

Priceless

NEARLY TIME FOR DINNER, KID!

LOOKS LIKE MOM'S ACTUALLY THE PERFECT VESSEL TO INHERIT THAT POWER.

## PICK YOUR POISON

DUR?!

EAT THIS.

Strand of hair.

UM, SO... THIS'LL TRANSFER THE POWER TO ME?

REALLY DOESN'T MATTER WHAT IT IS YOU EAT. AS LONG AS YOU GET MY DNA!!

FLINCH

JUST TRYING TO MAKE THIS EASY ON YOU.

I COULD ALWAYS GIVE YOU NAIL CLIPPINGS. OR EARWAX. OR BOOGERS...

HAIR, PLEASE.

OR A KISS?

GLARE

BEAM

## ALL MIGHT - HE'S JUST LIKE US!

I DID IT!!

HERE, TAKE A LOOK!!

ASTOUNDING! YOU'RE A REAL ENTER-TAINER! AND A TEEN, NO LESS!!

QUIVER

QUIVER

DELUXE COUPON

BOOTH FEE

100 YEN OFF

IT'S YOU, TEN MONTHS AGO.

WHAT'S THIS...?

ALL MIGHT HANGS OUT AT THOSE PLACES?

CRAP. HANG ON. THAT'S FOR MY NET CAFÉ.

TAP

TAP

## U.A. HIGH'S HERO COURSE!!

GRADUATES FROM U.A. ARE DESTINED TO BECOME GREAT HEROES!

WITH A CUTOFF SCORE OF 79, U.A. HIGH IS THE TOUGHEST HIGH SCHOOL IN THE NATION!!

AND SOME OTHERS WHO WE GOTTA OMIT!! NO ROOM!! BUT THEY'RE SWELL, TOO!!

THERE'S ALL MIGHT, WHO MAGNANI-MOUSLY DECLINED THE PEOPLE'S CHOICE AWARD!!

YES, THE KING OF THE COVETED 2 TO 3 A.M. SLOT, PRESENT MIC, IS HERE TO PRESENT THE EXAM GUIDELINES!!

MOST IMPOR-TANTLY, THE DUDE WHO WON THE JAPAN RADIO AWARD THREE YEARS IN A ROW... HOST OF "PUT YOUR HANDS UP RADIO"...

HELP!

YANK

HEY, HEY, SORRY 'BOUT THIS PARTY POOPER! AND WATCH THE THROAT, MAN! THAT'S MY MONEY-MAKER!!

AND YOU'RE AN EDUCATOR NOW, SO QUIT IT WITH THE SHILLING.

IF YOU'D CUT OUT THE GRAND-STANDING, YOU WOULDN'T HAVE HAD TO OMIT THE OTHERS.

## NO.3!!

MIDORIYA'S NEXT STEP TOWARDS BECOMING THE GREATEST HERO IS...

...U.A.'S ENTRANCE EXAM!!

IN $ WE TRUST

SO? HOW MUCH DOUGH DIDJA BRING?

HUH? MONEY? THE GUY AT THE FRONT DOOR TOOK IT ALL.

TELL IT TO SOMEONE WHO CARES.

SWEETS

POWER FROM ALL MIGHT IN HAND, HE IS ABOUT TO FACE HIS GREATEST CHALLENGE YET.

GUY AT THE FRONT DOOR

*MAY NOT REFLECT REALITY

## A DISH BEST SERVED COLD

KATSUKI BAKUGO.

IZUKU'S CHILDHOOD "FRIEND."

ALWAYS EXPLODING AT OUR LITTLE TRYHARD!!

BOOM

GET OUT OF MY WAY OR YOU'RE DEAD!!

K-KACCHAN!!

MOVE ASIDE, DEKU!!

DOESN'T MATTER WHO'S WHERE, SO STOP WASTING TIME.

ALL RIGHT. LINE UP, EXAMINEES.

SKF

!

LOUD-MOUTH. YOU'RE DONE. GO HOME.

DIDN'T I JUST SAY TO MOVE ASIDE?

UGH...

FWOOM

## 40 MINUTES IN TRANSIT

AFTER THAT I RUSHED HOME, PACKED MY BAG, AND HEADED FOR U.A.

I FINISHED MY TRAINING WITH ALL MIGHT...

BADUM BADUM

CAN'T BELIEVE ALL MIGHT HIMSELF COACHED ME LIKE THAT.

I'VE BEEN THROUGH SO MUCH THESE PAST TEN MONTHS.

BUT NOW YOU'VE GOT THE TICKET TO RIDE THE HERO TRAIN TO GREATNESS!!

A-ALL MIGHT...

THIS WAS THE LAST STEP OF YOUR TRAINING, KID!! ALL THAT'S LEFT IS TO STEP UP!!

PAT PAT

MY HERO ACADEMIA: VAGABOND ARC- BEGIN!!

THIS KID'S GOT ISSUES.

AWW, YER MAKING ME BLUSH.

THIS IS THE LAST STOP FOR THIS TRAIN, KID. ALL THAT'S LEFT IS TO STEP OFF.

DO YOU EVEN HAVE A TICKET FOR THIS TRAIN? HEY!

## SERIOUS BUSINESS

TENYA IDA.

ICON TO SERIOUS PEOPLE EVERYWHERE.

AN ELITE WHO GRADUATED FROM SOMEI MIDDLE SCHOOL.

EVERYBODY SAY "HEY"!!

WELCOME TO TODAY'S LIVE PERFORMANCE!!

SILENCE

JOLT

HEY.

HOW CAN HE SAY THAT WITH A STRAIGHT FACE?

Freaky...

YES. I AM POSITIVELY READY.

FWIP

ARE YOU READY?!

BADUM BADUM

## SIDE-EFFECTS MAY INCLUDE

DERP?!

FLOAT

ARE YOU OKAY?

OCHACO URARAKA.

QUIRK: ZERO GRAVITY.

ANYTHING SHE TOUCHES WILL BE UNAFFECTED BY GRAVITY! HOWEVER, USING HER POWER TOO MUCH MAKES HER QUEASY!!

IT'S MY QUIRK. SORRY FOR STOPPING YOU, BUT...

WELL, IT'S A BAD OMEN TO TRIP AND FALL.

PAT

AH.
Another one?!

SWOOSH

GUH-BWUH?!

D-DMP

Y-YOU OKAY? MORNING SICKNESS...? IS THE BABY MINE?

BADUM

HORK

URP...

BADUM

IN YOUR DREAMS...

## TRUE COLOR CONFESSIONS

THoOM

...OVERWHELMING THWOMP!

EACH TESTING SITE GETS A SINGLE, INDESTRUCTIBLE...

PEOPLE SHOW THEIR TRUE COLORS WHEN THEY FACE THAT THING. JUST LISTEN...

DASH

I'M ALWAYS PINCHING AND PRODDING MITSURU, BUT IT'S ONLY CUZ I LOVE HIM!!

WAHHH

I CALL MYSELF THE "FREE2PLAY LORD" BUT I ACTUALLY PAY FOR TONS OF MICROTRANSACTIONS!!

I SECRETLY SNIFF MY CLASSMATE'S DESK WHEN SHE GETS UP!

SORRY!!

I HABITUALLY BROWSE PORN ON MY DAD'S PHONE!!

BUT ALSO GOING TO HELL.

AT LEAST THEY'RE HONEST?

## NO EXPENSE SPARED

YOU'LL BE EXPERIENCING TEN-MINUTE-LONG "MOCK CITYSCAPE MANEUVERS"!!

C D E

CURRENT LOCATION

THIS IS HOW THE TEST WILL GO, MY LISTENERS!

BAM

IT'S LIKE A WHOLE CITY! HOW MANY OF THESE ARE ON THE GROUNDS?

SO BIG.

THAT'S U.A. FOR YA.

ALL THAT DETAIL, WHEN IT'S ALL JUST GONNA GET DESTROYED ANYWAY...

MEGA SMALL

BAM

THE HELL?! WE COULDN'T WRECK THE PLACE IF WE TRIED!!

CH-CHECK IT OUT!! THE LATEST TUNED MASS DAMPER ANTI-EARTHQUAKE TECH!!

## SMASHED EXPECTATIONS

...WHICH THEY EMPLOY IT AS A MOBILE EVACUATION SHELTER DURING EMERGENCIES.

WHEN NOT USED FOR TESTING, IT'S RENTED OUT TO INTERNATIONAL ORGANIZATIONS...

A KEY COMPONENT OF NATIONAL DEFENSE THAT RECEIVES 5% OF THE TOTAL MILITARY BUDGET!!

TOTAL COST: 240 BILLION YEN.

SMAASH

*ABOUT $2.4 BILLION

...AT NEXT YEAR'S BUDGET MEETING.

WAHHH

HOW COULD THIS HAPPEN?

WE'RE TOTALLY IN THE RED...

## DECISIONS, DECISIONS

OWW...

GWAH!

SHE'S THE GIRL WHO HELPED ME OUT THIS MORNING?!

HE'S THE BACKGROUND CHARACTER WHO COMMENTED ON HOW BIG THIS PLACE IS!!

OWW...

HOW DO I CHOOSE?

HUH?

# CHARACTER PROFILES!!

MY HERO ACADEMIA FEATURES SOME AWESOMELY FANTASTIC CHARACTERS, BUT HERE IN SMASH!!, THEIR GOOFBALL SETTING HAS BEEN DIALED UP TO 11! AS A RESULT, THEY ALSO GET NEW CHARACTER PROFILE PAGES!!

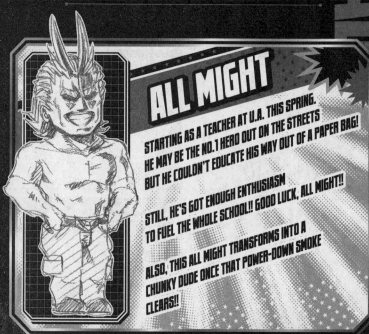

## ALL MIGHT

STARTING AS A TEACHER AT U.A. THIS SPRING. HE MAY BE THE NO. 1 HERO OUT ON THE STREETS BUT HE COULDN'T EDUCATE HIS WAY OUT OF A PAPER BAG!

STILL, HE'S GOT ENOUGH ENTHUSIASM TO FUEL THE WHOLE SCHOOL!! GOOD LUCK, ALL MIGHT!!

ALSO, THIS ALL MIGHT TRANSFORMS INTO A CHUNKY DUDE ONCE THAT POWER-DOWN SMOKE CLEARS!!

**RECOIL-ISH**

WHOA?!

...A-ALL MIGHT'S POWER?!

AMAZING... SO THIS IS...

GUH?!

SO FAST THAT YOUR BODY WILL BE IN CRISIS!!

YOU MAY BE A PROPER VESSEL NOW, BUT YOU WERE PUT TOGETHER IN A HURRY.

THROB

...HE MEANT A MIDLIFE CRISIS?!

BY CRISIS...

TWIST

**NO.4!!**

I MANAGED TO USE ALL MIGHT'S POWER, BUT...

SMIRK

...I'M STILL NOWHERE NEAR MASTERING IT.

THIS IS MY STARTING LINE!! I'M GONNA BE THE KING OF THE HEROES!!

*NOT QUITE HOW IT HAPPENED

## FROM GRANNY'S POCKETS

HERE, HAVE SOME GUMMIES. EAT UP.

WELL DONE. GOOD JOB ON THE TEST.

YOUTHFUL HEROINE: RECOVERY GIRL! (NURSING INSTRUCTOR)

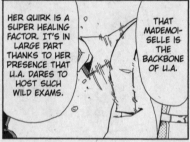

HER QUIRK IS A SUPER HEALING FACTOR. IT'S IN LARGE PART THANKS TO HER PRESENCE THAT U.A. DARES TO HOST SUCH WILD EXAMS.

THAT MADEMOISELLE IS THE BACKBONE OF U.A.

WELL DONE, ALL.

Um, thanks.

I USUALLY PREFER MY GUMMY BEARS WITH LESS POCKET LINT, BUT OKAY.

## MAKING EYES

CERTAIN DEATH? CAN'T HAVE THAT!!

THROB THROB THROB

AHH, I'M FALLING TO MY CERTAIN DEATH!!

?!

SLAM

ZERO GRAVITY

...TOUCHED A GIRL.*

I....

*ACTUALLY, SHE TOUCHED HIM, BUT OKAY.

SWOON

RELEASE

GWAHH!!

TUP

THUD

FWIP

UM... LIKE, EWW. NO THANKS!!

## HONOR SYSTEM

PLEASE BEGIN THE EXAM.

**BAM**

I MAY HAVE FALTERED DURING THE PRACTICAL EXAM, BUT I SHALL MAKE UP FOR IT WITH THE WRITTEN PORTION!! I HAVE MY SUPPLIES OUT, READY TO GO!

WRIT-TEN EXAM

**BAM**

SUPER eraser

D-DEAR ME...

?!

Translate the marked words into English.

Bob secretly sniffed Margaret's *keshigomu.* That night, with an expression of profound contentment on his [kao], he drifted off into deep, blissful [nemuri].

\* *KESHIGOMU = ERASER*

BATHROOM BREAK ALREADY?

**DOOM**

SHAKA

...

IT'S ON US FOR MISSING IT. JUST HAVE HIM FINISH THE TEST.

A GOOD THIRD OF THEM WOULD FAIL IF WE PUNISHED THEM FOR THAT.

HE CLAIMS HE CHEATED ON THE TEST.

ENGLISH TEACHER

WHO WROTE THAT QUESTION, ANYWAY?

## HELLOOO, NURSE

SO YOUR OWN BELOVED QUIRK DID THIS TO YOU...

**GRAND-MWAH!**

S M O O C H

?!

OVER HERE, MA'AM.

THIS ONE WILL BE FINE.

ANY OTHER HURT CHILDREN?

YAP

MY FIRST KISS...

S M O O C H

OKAY, NEXT!!

## KATSUKI'S RESULTS

THIS IS A PROJECTION!!

FOOM

!

CREAK

WHY ME, YOU ASK?! BECAUSE I'LL BE TEACHING AT U.A. STARTING THIS SPRING.

GOOD JOB ON THE TEST!! MY NAME IS ALL MIGHT.

GET TO THE POINT ALREADY.

TCH.

SLOW YOUR ROLL, KID. I WATCHED YOU IN ACTION, AND I CAN TELL YOU'RE THE IMPATIENT SORT.

AFTER ALL, HEROISM IS ALL ABOUT

WHAT'S THAT? YOU DON'T CARE? YOU JUST WANT TO HEAR YOUR RESULTS? HA HA HA!!

GRR

DID YOU GET IN, KATSUKI?

DUNNO.

CHAK

EH?

ZZZZ

## THE BAD OLD DAYS

WHERE'D YOU GO TO SCHOOL? IN THE CITY?

MAN, HIGH SCHOOL ENTRANCE EXAMS ARE THE PITS.

NAH. AN AGRI-CULTURAL SCHOOL UP IN HOKKAIDO.

AGRI-CULTURE?

IT'S FOR TIME ENTRANCE EXAMS

WE ONLY JUST RENOVATED THE SCHOOL BUILDING, SO...

I'M AFRAID WE CAN'T ACCOMMODATE HER QUIRK HERE.

HOW 'BOUT YOU KEEP WORKING HERE AFTER GRADUATION?

...

I'LL INTRODUCE YOU TO SOME SWELL SINGLE FELLAS.

GIRL, I TELL YA, LIFE'S BEEN EASY SINCE YOU CAME 'ROUND.

M OOO

EH? BAD MEMORIES?

SORRY... DUN WANNA TALK ABOUT IT.

| REALITY | FIRST IMPRESSIONS |
|---|---|

EVEN IF YOU PASSED THE WRITTEN PORTION ...

... NATURALLY RESULTS IN FAILURE.

...GETTING ZERO POINTS ON THE PRACTICAL...

PLEASE WATCH THE SCREEN!!

ALL MIGHT?! YOU'LL BE AT U.A.?!

BEEP

JOLT

A HERO COURSE THAT REJECTS THOSE WHO DO THE RIGHT THING IS NO HERO COURSE AT ALL!!

HOWEVER, WE WEREN'T JUST WATCHING FOR VILLAIN-BASED POINTS!!

AT LEAST HOWEVER MANY POINTS HE GAVE UP TRYING TO SAVE ME...!

SHE CAME TO SEE US RIGHT AFTER THE TEST.

CAN YOU GIVE HIM SOME OF THE POINTS I EARNED?

WHICH IS WHY YOU'LL BE EXEMPT ...

...FROM THE WRITTEN PORTION WHEN YOU TRY AGAIN NEXT YEAR!!

Z°

OM

SHE MEANS ME!!

YOU KNOW THE ONE? HE'S, UH, REALLY PLAIN LOOKING.

UM, THAT CURLY-HAIRED BOY... WITH FRECKLES...

SEE YOU NEXT YEAR, MIDORIYA, KID!!

THAT WAY, YOU CAN FOCUS ON BOOSTING THAT PRACTICAL SCORE!!

THAT KID, RIGHT. HE PROBABLY BUYS PROTECTIVE SLEEVES FOR HIS COMIC BOOKS.

I GUESS THAT'S ME?

OR THE SORT OF GUY WHO LINES UP FOR EXCLUSIVE MERCH AT CONS?

LOOKS LIKE THE TYPE WHO'D BE INTO DATING SIMS, Y'KNOW?

## CRAFTY CONTROL

I JUST... CAN'T WIELD IT.

ONE FOR ALL... MY BODY IS BROKEN AFTER A SINGLE PUNCH OR KICK...

BUT ONCE YOU FIGURE OUT HOW TO REGULATE THE POWER, YOU CAN PUT OUT JUST AS MUCH AS YOUR BODY CAN HANDLE.

THAT'S JUST HOW IT IS. FOR NOW, IT'S STILL ALL OR NOTHING.

FWIP

...THE BETTER YOU CAN *CONTROL* THE POWER!

THE MORE YOU *TEMPER* YOUR VESSEL...

BULGE

?

SNIP

SRIP

FWIP

ALL MIGHT!

TA-DA!

LIKE THIS.

CONGRATS ON PASSING

NO.5!!

I PASSED THE ENTRANCE EXAM, MADE IT INTO U.A....

...AND FOUND MYSELF SURROUNDED BY STUDENTS WITH KILLER QUIRKS.

I'M BOTH PUMPED AND NERVOUS TO START HIGH SCHOOL!

## SCHOOL RULES

U.A. HIGH BOASTS THE BIGGEST CAMPUS IN ALL OF JAPAN.

THIS PLACE IS HUGE.

1-A...
1-A...

...DESIGNED TO BE ACCESSIBLE TO ALL.

IT CONTAINS A VARIETY OF MULTI-USE FACILITIES...

YOU CAN EVEN DOWNLOAD AN EXCLUSIVE MAP APP.

THE OFFICIAL WEBSITE HAS A GUIDE TO THE BUILDINGS AND CLASS-ROOMS.

SWIPE
SWIPE

AND YOU GET ONE HECKUVA TELLING OFF FOR STEPPING ON SOMEONE ELSE'S SHOE.

BUT NO RUNNING IN THE HALLS ALLOWED.

Now's my chance.

SNEAK

## PRIORITIES

ENTRANCE CEREMONY DAY

AND YOUR HANDKERCHIEF?! HAVE YOU GOT THAT?!

YEP.

IZUKU! HAVE YOU GOT YOUR POCKET TISSUES?!

I'VE GOT IT!! NO TIME. GOTTA HURRY.

WHAT?!

IZUKU!

YOU FORGOT YOUR PANTS.

## ENTENDRE

## IDA AND KATSUKI

## A RATIONAL CREATURE

1-A'S HOMEROOM TEACHER IS A PRO HERO WHO LIVES LIFE RATIONALLY.

I'M YOUR HOMEROOM TEACHER, AIZAWA.

IF YOU'RE HERE TO SOCIALIZE, THEN GET OUT.

SURE THING, PRINCIPAL NEZU.

AIZAWA, CAN I ASK YOU TO RUN AN ERRAND IN THE NEXT TOWN OVER TOMORROW?

*THAT NIGHT*

IS THAT YOU, AIZAWA?!

UH... WAIT!

NO. MY PLACE IS IN THE OPPOSITE DIRECTION OF MY ERRAND TOMORROW. WASTE OF TIME TO GO HOME TONIGHT.

YEAH, OKAY, BUT LIKE, EVER HEARD OF A MOTEL?!

IS THIS WHERE YOU *LIVE*?

## ALL ABOUT MINETA

WITH A PERV IQ* OF 250, THIS PRODIGY CAN FIND THE DIRTY SIDE OF JUST ABOUT ANY SITUATION.

CLASS 1-A FEATURES ITS VERY OWN SELF-STYLED CASANOVA, MINORU MINETA.

*A NUMBER SIGNIFYING ONE'S CAPACITY FOR PERVITUDE*

A-ANOTHER TRIP TO THE NURSE'S OFFICE, HUH?

NOBODY'S IMAGINATION IS THAT GOOD!!

PLUS...

I JUST PICTURE HOW SHE MUST'VE LOOKED 50 YEARS AGO.

H-HE'S NOT NORMAL...

I ACCEPT ALL AGES, FROM CRADLE TO GRAVE.

## CAREER GOALS

...AND WILL BE *EXPELLED.*

THE ONE WITH THE LOWEST SCORE WILL BE JUDGED *HOPELESS*...

WELCOME. THIS IS...

YOUR FATES ARE IN OUR HANDS.

...THE HERO COURSE AT U.A. HIGH.

TEACHER LYFE

...TO BECOME A TEACHER AT ANY COST.

YES, THAT WAS THE MOMENT I DECIDED...

## A RATIONAL POLICY

NO TIME TO WASTE ON THAT STUFF IF YOU WANT TO BECOME HEROES.

A TEST OF OUR QUIRKS?! WHAT ABOUT THE ENTRANCE CEREMONY?! OR GUIDANCE SESSIONS?!

AIZAWA...

AS EXPECTED OF U.A.

TCH. THAT'S COOL I GUESS.

GRIP

SILENCE

ENTRANCE CEREMONY

HERO COURSE

SOUND SYSTEM IS SET TO GO!! YEAH!!

AHEM, ON THIS AUSPICIOUS DAY, WE GATHER TO...

CLASS A IS AWFULLY LATE.

READ THE ROOM, MIC.

## JARGON

THAT'S "PLUS ULTRA."

...U.A. WILL RUN YOU THROUGH THE WRINGER...

FOR THE NEXT THREE YEARS...

"PLUS ULTRA"! THAT MEANS "GO, BEYOND"! TOO COOL!!

BRING IT.

USE YOUR STRENGTH TO OVERCOME.

PLUS ULTRA TO THE LEFT.

HEY, WHERE SHOULD I SET UP THIS CONE?

'KAY.

SWURL

A LITTLE MORE ULTRA.

PLUS ULTRA THIS WAY?

THERE, PERFECT. JUST ULTRA.

FWP

## NO.6!!

AIZAWA SENSEI SAID THE LOWEST SCORER WILL BE EXPELLED!

BUT I CAN'T REGULATE MY POWER YET, AND A SINGLE USE TOTALLY DESTROYS MY BODY!

WHAT'LL I DO?!

*IT WASN'T NEARLY THIS DRAMATIC.

## CREATING VICTORY

...I CAN GUESS WHAT THEY'RE CAPABLE OF. AND WHAT THEY'RE NOT.

THEY'RE PUSHING THEIR QUIRKS TO THEIR LIMITS. BY SEEING HOW MUCH THEY'VE IMPROVED...

GRIP STRENGTH

1.2 TONS

28 KILOMETERS

BOOM

THROWING

MOMO YAOYOROZU.

QUIRK: CREATION.

SHE CAN CREATE ANY NONLIVING THING AS LONG AS SHE KNOWS ITS COMPOSITION.

I'LL ALLOW IT.

VROOM

ENDURANCE RUNNING

C'MON, THAT'S GOTTA BE A VIOLATION!!

## APPEARANCES (DON'T) MATTER

ZOOM

EVENT 1: 50-METER DASH

3.04 SECONDS!!

IT HAD TO BE THIRD GEAR FOR THE 50-METER.

PRETTY STRAIGHT-FORWARD! HE'S FAST!!

SKF

TENYA IDA.

QUIRK: ENGINE.

DRRR

HMPH

I SHALL EMERGE VICTORIOUS!!

ALL PERFECTLY SUITED TO MY QUIRK.

EVENT 4: SIDE-TO-SIDE STEPPING.

SHP

IT'S INSPIRING HOW LITTLE HE CARES ABOUT HOW DUMB HE LOOKS.

DRRR

HERE I GO!!

DRRR

# Snow White with the Red Hair

Story and Art by Sorata Akiduki

Shirayuki is an herbalist famous for her naturally bright-red hair, and the prince of Tanbarun wants her all to himself! Unwilling to become the prince's possession, she seeks shelter in the woods of the neighboring kingdom, where she gains an unlikely ally—the prince of that kingdom! He rescues her from her plight, and thus begins the love story between a lovestruck prince and an unusual herbalist.

SO YOU'RE SAYING HE WANTS A COMMONER LIKE ME AS HIS NEXT CONCUBINE JUST BECAUSE MY HAIR'S RED?

THE COURT ISN'T GOING TO LIKE THAT.

ARE YOU KIDDING ME?

IN ANY CASE, YOU'LL BE TAKEN TO THE CASTLE THREE DAYS FROM NOW. MAKE ANY PREPARATIONS YOU NEED.

IT DOESN'T MATTER WHO YOU ARE, SO LONG AS HE'S INTERESTED.

Doesn't matter who I am...?

I GUESS I CAN'T REFUSE.

THE PRINCE MAY BE AN INFAMOUS FOOL, BUT HE'S STILL A PRINCE...

T N K

SNIP

THIS IS THE PATH I CHOOSE.

AND I WON'T ALLOW...

GUESS I'VE GOT NO CHOICE...

GOOD DAY TO YOU, LADY SHIRAYUKI.

## GREETINGS

Hi there, I'm Sorata Akiduki.

So you somehow wound up with a copy of *Snow White with the Red Hair*.

This is my first published book. Thanks a lot for picking it up!

Sorata Akiduki (pen name)

Raised on a steady diet of manga in Aichi Prefecture. Born in March. Blood type is AB. Personal policy is to always watch the high school baseball telecasts during summer without running the AC. This policy is sometimes violated.

J—just some— times—

BUILD ONE YOUR- SELF THEN?

THERE'S A PATH TO THE SIDE THAT MOST PEOPLE WOULD NEVER FIND.

IT'S NEVER A BAD THING TO HAVE A HORSE TO GET AWAY IN A HURRY.

CHIRP

I WISH THIS PLACE HAD A STABLE.

Harsh—

HUP!

FSH

Huh?

SHK

?!

?!

ZEN ?!

GAH !!

THUD

TWO.

WHO'RE YOU, THOUGH?

IT'S ME, MITSU-HIDE!

!!

WHAT'S ONE PLUS ONE?!

BAM

AHH! ARE YOU OKAY, ZEN?! DIDJA SPRAIN YOUR ANKLE?! HIT YOUR HEAD?!

...

UGH...

I'M NOT TALKING ABOUT YOU GUYS.

YOU TOO, KIKI? HARSH.

AH! GOOD TO FINALLY LEARN HIS NAME.

CHK

!

AND WHAT'S BROUGHT YOU SO DEEP INTO THE WOODS?

SHOCK

...AND I'VE BEEN STAYING OFF THE MAIN ROADS.

I RAN AWAY FROM HOME...

WHO ARE YOU?

**AH!**

!!

Oh.

YOU'VE GOT MEDICINE?

I'VE GOT POULTICES AND THE LIKE ON ME.

I'M AN HERBAL-IST BY TRADE...

May I..?

HMPH!

DON'T BOTHER.

NEVER MIND ME. IT LOOKS LIKE YOU'VE HURT YOUR HAND.

Huh?

WHAT OF IT?

THAT'S SOME INTERESTING HAIR YOU'VE GOT THERE.

REALLY? I HEAR THAT A LOT.

UGH...

I'M NO IGNORANT PEASANT.

AND I'M NOT ABOUT TO TRUST A STRANGER JUST LIKE THAT.

FOR ALL WE KNOW THAT COULD BE POISON!

FW/P

GET IT? LEAVE US ALONE.

SO THANKS, BUT NO THANKS.

YOU WANNA FIGHT...?

Oh?

GRP

WH

?!

...

THROB

That hurt more than I thought it would!

AM

I MEAN, I UNDER-STAND HIS CON-CERNS.

BUT...

Watch it!

...

EVERYONE KEEPS TALKING DOWN TO ME...

...AND I'M GETTING REALLY SICK OF IT.

GO ON THEN. PLEASE.

UGH...

I'M SORRY.

SHF

AFTER ALL, IT KINDA WAS YOUR FAULT THAT I MESSED UP MY LANDING.

TRUE. WHATEVER YOU SAY GOES, I GUESS.

SEE?

No use in trying to stop him.

WE HANG OUT IN THIS VACANT HOUSE A LOT, SO...

...STAYING A FEW DAYS WON'T BE A PROBLEM.

RIGHT, KIKI? MITSU-HIDE?

SO MAKE IT RIGHT.

YOU'LL BE MY NURSE UNTIL I'M ALL HEALED, OKAY?

GRP

FROM ROYAL PALACE...

...TO THE WOODS...

LET'S HEAD INSIDE.

Make it right...?

LOOK! WE'RE FELLOW BANDAGE BUDDIES.

DON'T BE SO STUB- BORN.

Ha ha ha! We match, right?

...

IT'S FUNNY. LAUGH.

...THAT I'M *NOT* HAPPY ABOUT YOU KEEPING IT A SECRET, SHIRAYUKI.

WHAT I *SAID* WAS...

YOU WON'T BE HAPPY KNOWING THE REASON I RAN AWAY.

I KEEP TELLING YOU!

WHAT SORT OF GENTLEMAN WOULD LET AN INJURED GIRL WANDER AROUND THE WOODS ON HER OWN?

DID YOU HAVE TO FOLLOW ME, ZEN?

I'M GOING OUT FOR A WALK.

KIKI, MITSU-HIDE!

BEAM

Sure!

YOU TWO PLAY NICE, OKAY?

I'LL EVEN PUT UP WITH YOUR KEEPING SECRETS!

DROOP

HMPH!

Sigh...

I'M USED TO THE GREAT OUTDOORS FROM MY HERBALIST TRAINING.

TUG

YEAH.

I GET THAT.

TIME AND SPACE FLOW DIFFERENTLY OUTSIDE THE CITY.

IT PUTS ME AT EASE.

WAS THAT YOU OPENING UP JUST NOW?

!

HUH?

COULD I ASK YOU TO CUT IT FOR ME, ZEN?

Can't get loose...

I MUST'VE MISSED A SPOT BEFORE I LEFT HOME...

F S H

OWW ?!

...!

GRIN

HUH?

Ow, ow, ow...

YOUR HAIR SNAGGED ON A TREE. WHY'S THERE JUST ONE LONG LOCK BACK THERE?

OH.

YOU'RE UNBELIEV-ABLE.

I MIGHT BE INCLINED TO HELP, IN EXCHANGE FOR AN EXPLANA-TION...

BUT WHAT'S CHOPPING OFF YOUR HAIR GOT TO DO WITH LEAVING HOME?

NO WAY! ME, CUT A LADY'S HAIR? NEVER!

He cut it for her.
↓

HE'S A FAMOUS MAN WHO LEARNED HIS MANNERS IN BROTHELS AND EATS WITH GOLD CUTLERY.

...AND THAT WAS ENOUGH TO MAKE HIM INTERESTED IN ME.

MY RED HAIR IS RARE...

Speech-less!

SOME RICH BOY DEMANDED THAT YOU BECOME HIS CONCUBINE ?!

SO...

SHIRA—

...I'D BE NO MORE THAN AN APPLE HE BOUGHT AT THE MARKET.

IF I AGREED ...

...I LEFT HIM A BUNDLE OF MY HAIR...

...TO STARE AT UNTIL HE'S SICK OF IT.

CLASSIC!!

HA HA HA HA HA HA!

PFFT!!

IT'S REALLY NO LAUGHING MATTER.

THEY SAY...

...THAT RED IS THE COLOR OF DESTINY.

NAH, I MEAN...

GOOD CHOICE!

?

GIVING THE SLIP TO A SLEAZE LIKE THAT.

YOU'RE HAVING A HARD TIME NOW, BUT...

...GOOD THINGS COME WHEN YOU LEAST EXPECT THEM.

WE MIGHT'VE FOUND A FORCE OF NATURE...

....IN THIS SHIRA-YUKI.

SHIRAYUKI REALLY DOESN'T SEEM SUSPICIOUS. RIGHT, KIKI?

HARDLY. IN FACT, I THINK ZEN IS INTO HER.

OH? SO YOU'RE FINALLY STARTING TO RE-SPECT ME?

HUH...

THAT WAS REALLY DEEP...

DELIVERY FROM TANBARUN!

HUH?!

FWUMP

FROM THE NEXT KINGDOM OVER? TO HERE OF ALL PLACES...?

FROM TANBARUN, REALLY?

...Here, it's quite heavy.

...THE RIBBON I TIED AROUND THE HAIR I CUT!

THAT'S...

....!

?

HUH?!

GRP

SHIRA-YUKI?

LOOKS LIKE...

...THE GUY WHO SENT THIS GOT WORRIED WHEN HE SAW YOU'D LEFT HOME.

AND HE'S WAITING FOR YOU IN THE TOWN ON TANBARUN'S BORDER...

A PERSISTENT GENTLEMAN, ISN'T HE?

Ha ha!

THAT'S ONE WAY TO PUT IT.

WHY CROSS THE BORDER AND GO TO SUCH LENGTHS TO GET AWAY?!

WHAT'S SO FUNNY?!

CAN I LOOK AT WHAT'S INSIDE?

URK

HUH?

SURE...

APPLES...

...

MAYBE THE APPLES ARE POISONED?

SO HE'S A MAN WHO SEES WHAT HE WANTS...

...AND ASSUMES IT'S ALREADY HIS.

Not surprised.

HUH ...?

JUST KIDDING.

SHF

TMP

ZEN?

CHOMP

WOW.

HARSH!

GET OUT! I DIDN'T SUMMON YOU!!

S...

STOP SPYING!

K OFF

WHERE ARE YOUR MANNERS, ZEN?

Get your own apple.

WHAT?!

UM, ZEN.

UGH...

...

K L TTR

...

K OFF!

!!

ZEN—

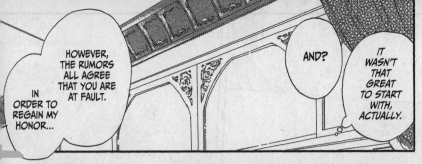

HOWEVER, THE RUMORS ALL AGREE THAT YOU ARE AT FAULT.

IN ORDER TO REGAIN MY HONOR...

AND?

IT WASN'T THAT GREAT TO START WITH, ACTUALLY.

...I NEED YOU TO AGREE TO BECOME MY CONCUBINE.

I'D RATHER NOT HAVE YOU SHAMED, COMMONER OR NOT.

SO I PAIN-STAKINGLY ARRIVED AT THIS AMICABLE SOLUTION.

...I STUMBLED UPON JUST THE THING TO MAKE YOU SAY YES.

AS LUCK WOULD HAVE IT...

AH!

YOU'RE JOKING...

AM I HEARING THIS RIGHT?!

WHY NOT BRING ONE...

...TO YOUR AILING FRIEND AS A GET-WELL GIFT, LADY SHIRAYUKI?

SHP...

I WOULD HATE...

...TO HAVE SOMEONE SO VERY EASY ON THE EYES...

...BE THE ONE THAT GOT AWAY.

ROLL

"THEY SAY THAT RED..."

"...IS THE COLOR OF DESTINY."

BAAAM

I OBJECT!!

GASP!

?!

WH-WHO ARE YOU?

ZEN?!

WHERE'S MY GUARD?

...SPEWING STUPID GARBAGE INTO THAT GIRL'S EAR.

STOP...

TMP

HUH?

ZEN...!!

W-WAIT! HOW ARE YOU UP AND ABOUT...?

It came loose.

MIND TYING THIS FOR ME?

HEYA, SHIRA-YUKI.

DON'T YOU WORRY.

WE'RE KEEPING WATCH NOW.

!!

WHAT TERRIBLE LUCK!

SO YOU'RE THE JERK BEHIND THE APPLES?

IT WAS MEANT TO KNOCK OUT LADY SHIRAYUKI SO SHE COULD BE BROUGHT TO ME. BUT, ALAS...

OH. WELL, EXCUUUSE ME...

...YOUR GREAT LORDLI-NESS.

...WHEN SPEAKING TO YOUR BETTERS.

Hmph!

MIND YOUR MAN-NERS...

!

WURL

I SEE.

YOU MUST BE THE MAN WHO GOT POISONED!

...

WURL

THAT SAID...

...I NEVER EXPECTED AN ATTEMPT ON MY LIFE BY A NEIGHBORING ROYAL...

...PRINCE RAJ.

HE LOOKS ILL...

IT...

IT'S TRUE! I SAW THE CREST ON THEIR BELONG-INGS...

RIGHT, MISTER?

IT'S ALL TRUE.

THEN LET'S MAKE A DEAL, OH IDIOT PRINCE.

MAYBE WE NEED A PUBLIC HEARING TO EXPOSE THE TRUTH?

ACK!!

NO...

HMPH!

Y-YOU... UH, YOU HAVE NO PROOF THAT I'M THE POISONER!

SCARED!

WE'VE GOT PLENTY, ACTUALLY.

YOUR ATTITUDE, AND THE THINGS IN THIS ROOM EVEN.

WE'LL KEEP YOUR FOOLISHNESS A SECRET. BUT IN EXCHANGE...

SWEAR TO ME THAT YOU WON'T EVEN SPEAK HER NAME AGAIN.

...YOU'LL LEAVE SHIRAYUKI ALONE. FOREVER.

THIS IS YOUR CHANCE TO LET HIM HAVE IT.

Huh?

I'M SURE YOU'VE GOT PLENTY TO SAY TO HIM.

SHIRA-YUKI!

LADY SHIRA-YUKI? BUT WHY?

NEED ME TO DRAW MY SWORD?

CHAK

TMP

Go on.

RIGHT.

GRP

FINE! I SWEAR! I SWEAR IT!!

ALSO...

2 CM

YOU dropped it.

YOUR GET-WELL GIFT.

HERE, PRINCE RAJ.

FWIP

GIVE THE ANTI-DOTE...

...TO ZEN. NOW!

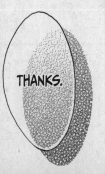

THANKS.

FROM NOW ON, I'LL HAVE MITSUHIDE PEEL ALL MY FRUIT FIRST.

YOU'RE KINDA MISSING THE POINT!

ENOUGH, I GET IT ALREADY!

SORRY.

WE THREE WEREN'T VIGILANT ENOUGH. THAT'S ALL!

MITSUHIDE WAS EVEN CRYING HIS EYES OUT, SAYING HE'D FOLLOW ZEN IN DEATH.

RELAX, SHIRAYUKI. DON'T BE SORRY.

ZEN ATE THE APPLE ALL ON HIS OWN.

Kiki!

...BACK IN THE WOODS?

YOU REMEM- BER WHAT I SAID...

SHIRA- YUKI.

KLTR

THE TWO OF US...

...BEING TOGETHER LIKE THIS...

I'D BE THRILLED IF IT TURNS OUT TO BE DESTINY.

YOU REALLY HAVE AN INTERESTING WAY OF THINKING.

...

OH, ZEN...

So dramatic!

Right?

WHAT?

IT'S A WAY OF LIVING.

NOT "THINK-ING."

SHif

THIS IS...

...MY OWN TALE.

SHIRAYUKI?

WHAT'S YOUR ANSWER?

WHAT LIES BEYOND THIS ENCOUNTER, IF THIS IS THE PATH I CHOOSE?

I KNOW WHAT I'LL CHOOSE...

THE SOUND OF MY STORY'S PAGES ARE TURNING...

...LIKE SO MANY ECHOING FOOTSTEPS...

WE'LL BE IN TROUBLE TOO.

NO HAPPILY EVER AFTER HERE.

We've been away for days now...

Oh?

...YOU SHOULD KNOW, SHIRAYUKI... ZEN'S "DESTINY" IS TO GET A GOOD SCOLDING WHEN WE GET BACK TO THE PALACE.

HE'S PLAYING IT COOL NOW, BUT...

# Urusei Yatsura
### Story and Art by Rumiko Takahashi

Welcome to the original supernatural harem series, written by Eisner Hall of Fame inductee and manga legend Rumiko Takahashi.

Beautiful space alien princess Lum invades Earth on her UFO, and unlucky Ataru Moroboshi's world gets turned upside down! Will Lum become Earth's electrifying new leader? Or will Ataru somehow miraculously save Earth from space alien onslaught?

I HATE YOU!!

WHY? ALL I DID WAS GLANCE AT ANOTHER WOMAN!

I NEVER WANT TO SPEAK TO YOU AGAIN!

SHINOBU!!

HUH?!

WAHH! WAIT, WAIT, WAIT!!

GAH!!

WOMP

DON'T DO IT!!

TMP TMP TMP TMP

WHO KILLS THEMSELVES JUST BECAUSE THEY GOT DUMPED?!

YOU WEREN'T PLANNING ON JUMPING?! LIAR!

I'M TOO LATE...

OH DEAR.

WHAT WAS THAT FOR?!

SPLASH

AND WOUND UP PUSHING ME IN?!

I SAW THE SHADOW OF DEATH ON YER BACK! I WAS TRYIN' TO SAVE YA...

BUT I LIVE IN THAT DIRECTION!

TROUBLE LIES IN THAT DIRECTION!

WAIT! DON'T GO THAT-AWAY!

I'VE HAD IT! I'M GOING HOME!

...IS HORRIBLE!

YER...YER FACE...

AN EVIL SPIRIT? PLEASE!

YER FACE IS POSSESSED BY AN EVIL SPIRIT!

LIKE AN OGRE OR AN ALIEN? BRING IT ON!

...YER FEATURES PORTEND BAD LUCK!

WHAT I MEAN TO SAY IS...

WELL, WHY DIDN'T YOU JUST SAY THAT, THEN?

HUH? WHAT'S GOING ON? THAT'S MY HOUSE...

CAN WE GET A COMMENT, PLEASE?

ARE YOU ATARU MOROBOSHI?

WHAT? IS THAT THE BOY?!

OH! THE MOROBOSHI BOY IS HOME!

YOU'LL SEE!!

DID SOMETHING HAPPEN?

ATARU!!

WHAT'S GOING ON, MOM?

OH MY! YOU MEAN YOU DON'T KNOW?!

THE WORLD'S ATTENTION IS FOCUSED ON YOU RIGHT NOW!

WHAT'S THIS ALL ABOUT?

YOU'D BETTER MEET YOUR GUEST.

IS SOME-ONE HERE?

I WAS SO WOR-RIED!

I HEARD THE NEWS...

ATARU!

ATARU! YOU'RE HOME!

SHINOBU? WHAT ARE YOU DOING HERE?

BRACE MYSELF?! WHAT'RE YOU TALKING ABOUT—

BRACE YOURSELF!

WELCOME HOME!

GAH!!

YEP!

I'M THE CHOSEN ONE?!

WE'RE TO DO BATTLE WITH A HUMAN RANDOMLY SELECTED BY OUR COMPUTER. IF WE LOSE, WE GO HOME!

THEY'RE INVADING EARTH. THERE'S ONLY ONE POSSIBLE CONDITION FOR SALVATION...

YEAH! BEGONE, OGRE!

NO! ATARU CAN'T FIGHT AN OGRE! HE'LL DIE!

DON'T GLOAT ABOUT IT!

TOLDJA THERE WAS AN EVIL SPIRIT ON YA!

THIS IS MY OPPONENT?!

WE'RE PLAYING TAG?!

OH!

NOW AN OGRE'S CALLING ME AN OGRE?!

YOU'RE THE OGRE!

THE BATTLE IS A GAME OF TAG!

*SAKURANBO MEANS CHERRY IN JAPANESE.

DID YOU COME HERE TO MAKE STUPID PUNS?!

CALL ME CHERRY.

BROTHER SAKURAN-BO?

I'M A TRAVELING MONK. MY NAME IS SAKURAN-BO.*

YES. AT FIRST GLANCE HE LOOKS PERFECTLY ORDINARY, BUT HE BEARS THE MARK OF AN EXTREMELY UNLUCKY STAR!

ARE HIS FEATURES REALLY UNLUCKY?

YOU WANTED TO TELL US SOMETHING ABOUT ATARU'S FACE?

IT WAS AN UNLUCKY DAY ACORDING TO THE JAPANESE CALENDAR TOO!

DID YOU REALIZE, DEAR, THAT ATARU WAS BORN ON A FRIDAY THE 13TH?

WELL ... LET'S SEE ...

AS HIS PARENTS, DID YOU HAVE ANY INKLING?

WELL, OUR FAMILY ALTAR FELL OVER! I WAS TERRIFIED!

AND WHEN YOU PANICKED AND TRIED TO RUN TO SAFETY, YOU BROKE THE STRAP OF YOUR SANDALS...

THAT'S ENOUGH!

ALMOST ALL OF OUR TEACUPS BROKE!

AND AN EARTHQUAKE STRUCK JUST AS HE LET OUT HIS FIRST CRY!

CRAP!

DASH

IT'S DAY EIGHT, AND NIGHTFALL IS APPROACHING...

BOTH CONTESTANTS ARE SHOWING SIGNS OF FATIGUE!

WHAT'RE YOU DOING, YOU PERV?!

RRRRM

WHAM!

HUH?!

YAY!

AIEEE!!

GRAB

HE DID IT!!

THUD

TWENTY-
TWO!

TWENTY-
ONE!

GIVE
IT
BACK!

HOW LONG
HAVE YOU
BEEN
THERE?!

THE THING
YOU STOLE
FROM ME!

GIVE
WHAT
BACK
?!

THE GAME OF
TAG IS ONLY
ON BETWEEN
DAWN AND
DUSK!

IF YOU
WANT IT,
COME AND
GET IT!

WHAT,
THIS?

YOU'RE
WEARING
IT?!

FINE!!

YOU
CAME
TO GET
THIS
BACK,
RIGHT?

GIVE IT BACK!!

NO WAY!!

AAAH!!

HE'S EVEN PRACTICING YELLING!

HE SURE IS TRAINING HARD!

TAKE THAT!!

SHE DOESN'T HAVE A SPARE ONE...

MY LUCK IS FINALLY CHANGING...

HEY LOOK! OOH

EEK!!

SNATCHING— ER, SEIZING— LUM'S BRASSIERE YESTERDAY SEEMS TO HAVE BOOSTED MOROBOSHI'S CONFIDENCE! HE'S FULL OF RENEWED ENERGY!

YEAH! YEAH! YEAH! WOO! YEAH! YAY!

YOU'VE GOT THIS TODAY!

I KNEW IT! SHE CAN'T USE HER ARMS SO HER JUMPS ARE WEAKER...

HOP

TUP

HMPH!

ALL RIGHT— LET'S TRY THIS AGAIN!

TMP

VOOSH

GROWL

YEEK!!

GRAB

IN OTHER WORDS, VICTORY IS MINE!!

VSH

ATARU!

ATARU!

**YAY!**

ATARU!!

HOORAY! ATARU MOROBOSHI HAS SAVED THE EARTH!!

HUH ?!

FINE! IF YOU WANT IT THAT BADLY, I'LL MARRY YOU!

*HEE HEE HEE!* NOW WE CAN FINALLY GET MARRIED!

CON-GRATULA-TIONS, MORO-BOSHI!

WELL DONE!

H R K K ?!

COME TO THINK OF IT, HE WAS SHOUTING SOMETHING ABOUT MARRIAGE THROUGHOUT THE COMPETITION TODAY!

WOW! MOROBOSHI IS GOING TO MARRY LUM?!

IF SHE WANTS TO MARRY YOU, WHY DON'T YOU GO FOR IT?!

WHAT'S YOUR DEAL? HOW LONG ARE YOU GOING TO CLING TO HER LIKE THAT?

SHINOBU!!

HMPH!

WAIT! HE PROPOSED TO ME!

LET'S GO, LUM. WE LOST.

SHI-NO-BU!!

THIS IS TOO MUCH! AFTER ALL THAT?!

GET AWAY FROM ME, YOU PLAYER!

HE'LL MAKE A GOOD HUSBAND!

ATARU! BE SURE YOU COME HOME FOR OBON FESTIVAL AND NEW YEAR'S!

DESTINY WILLS IT TO BE THUS!

SHINOBU!!

A SECRET PASSION... MUST'VE BEEN ROUGH!

THIS IS A DISASTER!

A GOODWILL MARRIAGE— TO UNITE OUR WORLDS!

IF YOU WANT TO MARRY LUM, YOU'LL HAVE TO COME LIVE ON OUR PLANET!

G A C K!!

WE'LL GET YOU A PAIR OF HORNS AND MAKE A PROPER OGRE OF YOU!

# Beastars

Story and Art by Paru Itagaki

At a high school where the students are literally divided into predators and prey, it's personal relationships that maintain the fragile peace. Who among them is a Beastar—a hero destined to become a leader in a society naturally rife with mistrust?

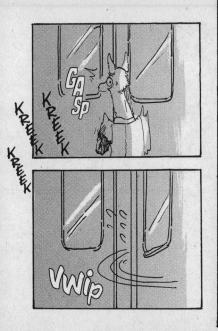

BECAUSE
THIS IS
YOUR
TRUE
NATURE
...?

WE
KNOW...

SOME-
WHERE
DEEP
IN OUR
HEARTS,
WE
ALWAYS
KNOW...

Aiee!

**B A M**

COULD IT BE THAT ...?

I G-GET IT NOW. YOU NEVER ...

...

**B A M**

... REALLY THOUGHT OF US AS EQUALS, DID YOU?!

**B A M**

TO CARNI-VORES LIKE YOU...

... WE'RE JUST ...

...FOOD!

...

BUT YOU'RE WRONG.

...SO MUCH LEFT TO DO...

Cherryton Academy

HEY, ANON! THE RUMOR'S TRUE...

I CAN'T BELIEVE IT... HE WAS HANGING OUT WITH US JUST YESTERDAY...

THE VICTIM WAS TEM!

IT'S SO EARLY IN THE MORNING...

W- WHAT HAP- PENED ?!

...IN LEC- TURE ROOM TWO...

AN ALPACA BOY NAMED TEM WAS FOUND DEAD...

THE POLICE THINK A CARNIVORE WHO GOES HERE...

...KILLED HIM.

Drama Club Correspondence Notebook

A-ARE YOU IMPLYING THAT ONE OF US...?!

THAT GREY WOLF LEGOSHI IS ONE OF YOUR ROOMMATES, RIGHT? GIVE HIM THIS NOTEBOOK.

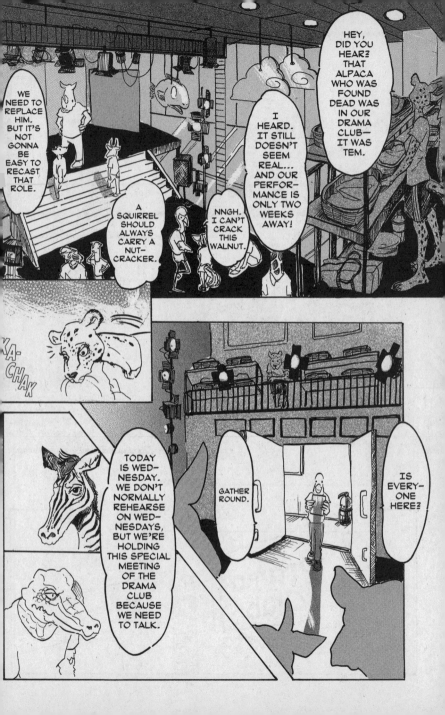

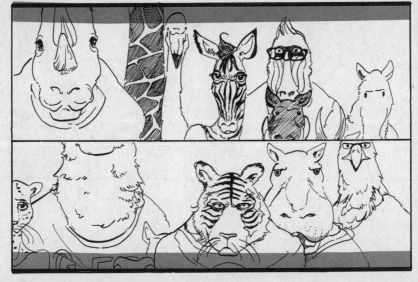

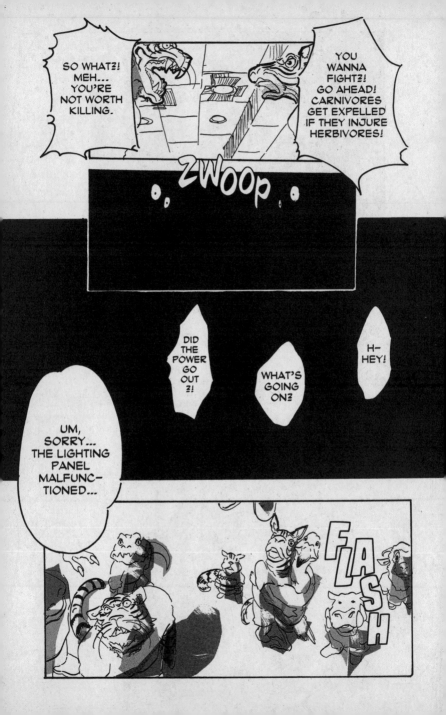

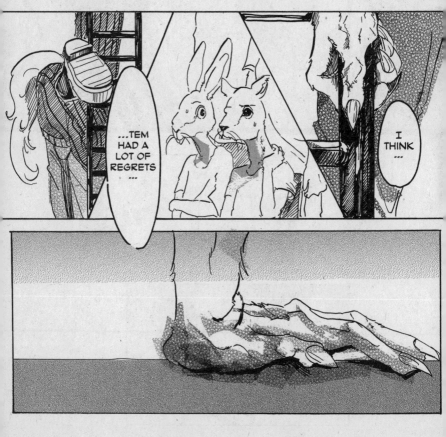

...BECAUSE THERE WERE SO MANY THINGS... HE DIDN'T GET A CHANCE TO DO YET.

H-HOW WOULD YOU KNOW?

...

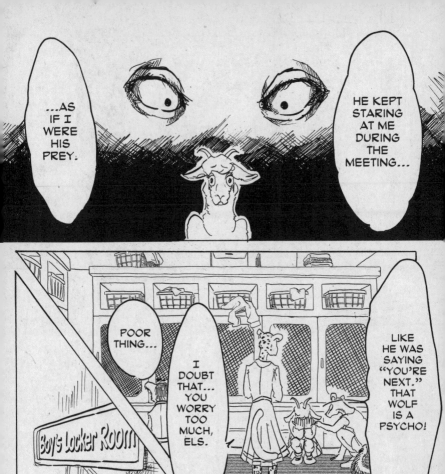

...AS IF I WERE HIS PREY.

HE KEPT STARING AT ME DURING THE MEETING...

POOR THING...

I DOUBT THAT... YOU WORRY TOO MUCH, ELS.

LIKE HE WAS SAYING "YOU'RE NEXT." THAT WOLF IS A PSYCHO!

Boy's Locker Room

WHY DID WE HAVE TO FIGHT ON THE DAY ONE OF OUR MEMBERS DIED?! IS THIS HOW OUR AWARD-WINNING DRAMA CLUB RESPONDS TO TRAGEDY?!

I'LL GO STRAIGHT BACK TO MY DORM...

TEE HEE! THANKS. SEE YOU TOMORROW.

SEE YOU TOMORROW. AND YOU CAN ALWAYS DROP BY OUR ROOM IF YOU FEEL ANXIOUS AGAIN. WE PROSIMIANS ARE CHEERFUL AND FUN TO HANG OUT WITH!

IT PROBABLY HAPPENED RIGHT AROUND THIS TIME YESTERDAY.

I CAN'T IMAGINE HOW TERRIFIED TEM MUST HAVE BEEN WHEN HE GOT ATTACKED.

OF COURSE I'M... SAD...

...

ARE YOU SAD?

HOW COULD I! MY BOYFRIEND GAVE IT TO ME!

I MUST HAVE LEFT IT IN THE REHEARSAL ROOM.

OOPS, I FORGOT MY WATCH!

NO, IT WOULD HAVE BEEN MUCH LATER IN THE NIGHT...

EVERY-ONE LEFT THEIR STUFF LYING AROUND ...

IT'S PITCH-DARK... DID I LEAVE IT ON THE STAGE?

--- WHAT ARE YOU DOING HERE, ELS?

FLASH

YOU DIDN'T EVEN TURN THE LIGHTS ON.

W-WHY ARE *YOU* HERE, LEGOSHI?

I NEEDED TO BE ALONE WITH YOU.

I FOLLOWED YOU WHEN I SAW YOU WERE HEADING BACK TO THE REHEARSAL ROOM.

I'LL BE DONE SOON.

DON'T BE AFRAID.

NOW COME HERE...

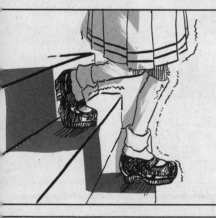

FORGIVE ME, TEM.

I DIDN'T FULLY GET IT UNTIL NOW.

YOU MUST HAVE BEEN PETRIFIED...

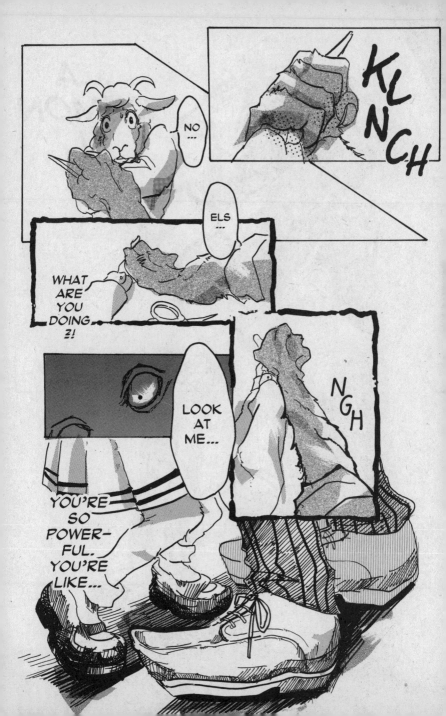

...I'M ABOUT TO...

I CAN'T BELIEVE...

...DIE!

FWAPPA

I'M SORRY. MAYBE I SHOULDN'T HAVE GIVEN YOU THE LETTER.

YEAH.

...YOU DIDN'T KNOW ABOUT IT.

BUT IT WOULD HAVE BEEN HARD TO PRETEND...

I SEE...

I THOUGHT TEM WOULDN'T WANT ANYONE ELSE TO FIND OUT. SO I WANTED TO GIVE IT TO YOU IN PRIVATE.

FWOOSH

YOU'RE AWKWARD...

YOU FRIGHT-ENED ME. BUT... I'M GRATE-FUL.

...BUT SWEET.

I'LL TREASURE THIS LETTER.

YES, SEE YOU.

I'M SORRY ABOUT TODAY. SEE YOU TOMOR-ROW.

UM ...

HEY !

I D-DON'T WANT THE OTHER DRAMA CLUB MEMBERS TO MISUNDERSTAND YOU.

B-BUT...

I'LL BE FINE. IT'S ALWAYS BEEN LIKE THIS. I'M USED TO BEING FEARED AND HATED. I'LL SURVIVE.

...UNTIL HE DISAPPEARED INTO THE NIGHT.

I WATCHED HIM GO, THE SLUMP OF HIS SHOULDERS BETRAYING HIS SORROW AT THE DEATH OF HIS FRIEND...

THE NIGHT BREEZE IN SPRINGTIME IS STILL COLD...

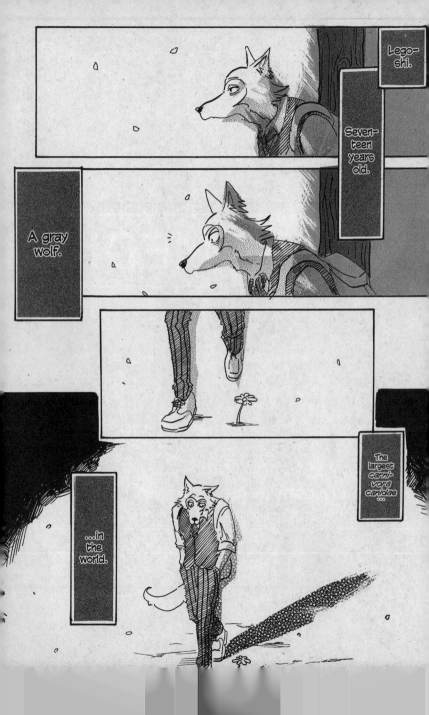

Lego-shi.

Seven-teen years old.

A gray wolf.

The largest carni-vora canidae...

...in the world.